EAT YOUR ROSES

EAT YOUR ROSES

... Pansies, Lavender and 49 other Delicious Edible Flowers

Denise Schreiber

st. lynn's press

PITTSBURGH

Eat Your Roses
…Pansies, Lavender and 49 Other Delicious Edible Flowers

Copyright © 2011 Denise Schreiber

ISBN-13: 978-0-981961-5-5-2

Library of Congress Control Number: 2010937021
CIP information available upon request

First Edition, 2011

St. Lynn's Press . POB 18680 . Pittsburgh, PA 15236
412.466.0790 . www.stlynnspress.com

Typesetting–Holly Rosborough, Network Printing Services
Cover Design–Jeff Nicoll
Editor–Catherine Dees

Food Photos © Patricia Toth McCormick
Flower Photo Credits are shown on the following page.

Disclaimer: The author and publisher expressly disclaim any responsibility for any adverse effects occurring as a result of the suggestions or information herein, including the handling or consuming of plants named in this book.

Printed in Malaysia by Tien Wah Press

This title and all of St. Lynn's Press books may be purchased for educational, business, or sales promotional use. For information please write:
Special Markets Department . St. Lynn's Press . POB 18680 . Pittsburgh, PA 15236

10 9 8 7 6 5 4 3 2 1

FLOWER PHOTO CREDITS

Note: Many of these photographs are from Creative Commons. In some cases a full name was provided for crediting, in other cases only a username. We wish to thank all the photographers listed below for the use of their images.

Anise hyssop: Wayne Ray
Apple blossom: audriusa
Artichoke: chinacrisis
Bachelor button/Cornflower: Teun Spaans
Basil: Michael Castielli
Borage: Victor M. Vicente Selvas
Broccoli: Rasbak
Calendula: H. Zell
Cauliflower: © Patricia Toth McCormick
Chamomile: Joaquim Alves Gaspar
Chive flower: © Patricia Toth McCormick
Dandelion: Sandy Feather
Daylily: Denise Schreiber
Dianthus: Zeynel Cebeci
Eastern redbud: Sandy Feather
Elderberry: J.M. Garg
False Red Yucca flower (hesperaloe): miwasatoshi
Fennel flower: Carsten Niehaus
Garlic scape: Canterel
Rose geranium: Laitche
Herbes de Provence: French Tart-FT
   (http://www.flickr.com/photos/frenchtart/)
Hibiscus: Andrew Fogg
Lavender: Denise Schreiber
Lemon balm: Nabokov
Lemon verbena: istock, N. Nehring
Lilac: Victor Lee

Signet Marigold: Goku122
Marjoram: Raul654
Mint, Spearmint: miguel303xm
Monarda/bee balm: Joe Schneid
Nasturtium: © Patricia Toth McCormick
Onion flower: © Patricia Toth McCormick
Orange blossom: Ellen Levy Finch
Oregano flower: Christian Bauer
Pansy: © Patricia Toth McCormick
Passionflower: Density
Garden Pea flower: Dyorkey
Pineapple guava: John Harrison
Pineapple Sage: Eric Hunt
Prickly pear: Denise Schreiber
Radish flower: Denise Schreiber
Rosemary: Christian Bauer
Roses: © Patricia Toth McCormick
Garden sage: Topjabot
Scarlet Runner Bean: Fatrabbit
Squash flower: jake7401
Strawberry: Sedum
Sunflower seeds, flower: © Patricia Toth McCormick
Tulip: Anslaton
Thyme flower: © Patricia Toth McCormick
Viola: Jjron
Yucca filimentosa: Meneerke bloem

TABLE OF CONTENTS

Introduction i
Rules for eating edible flowers iii
What flowers are NOT edible? iv
Gathering flowers & preparing them for use v

EDIBLE FLOWERS

Anise hyssop 2
Apple blossom 3
Artichoke 4
Bachelor button 5
Basil 6
Borage 7
Broccoli 8
Calendula 9
Cauliflower 10
Chamomile 11
Chive 12
Dandelion 13
Daylily 14
Dianthus 15
Eastern redbud 16
Elderberry 17
False red yucca 18
Fennel 19
Garlic, Garlic scapes 20
Geranium (Lime & Rose) 21
Herbes de Provence 22
Hibiscus 23
Lavender 24
Lemon balm 25
Lemon verbena 26
Lilac 27

Signet marigold 28
Marjoram 29
Mint 30
Monarda/bee balm 31
Nasturtium 32
Onion flower 33
Orange blossom 34
Oregano 35
Pansy 36
Passionflower 37
Pea, garden 38
Pineapple guava 39
Pineapple sage 40
Prickly pear 41
Radish 42
Rose 43
Rosemary 45
Sage, garden 46
Scarlet runner bean 47
Squash flower 48
Strawberry 49
Sunflower 50
Thyme 51
Tulip 52
Viola 53
Yucca 54

TABLE OF CONTENTS

RECIPES
Accents...56
Appetizers & Side Dishes...60
Salads...65
Entrees..69
Desserts..74
Drinks...78
Butters..81
Syrups...83
Sugars..86

Resources.. 87

Index 88

Acknowledgments 90

About the author 91

Eating flowers is one of the true pleasures in life, providing sustenance to our senses and renewing our joy in food.

I discovered the world of edible flowers back in 1999, when two friends and I decided to go to England and Wales to visit the famous gardens there. Joanne was a horticulture professor, Michele a landscape architect from Longwood Gardens, and I was greenhouse manager for Western Pennsylvania's Allegheny County Parks. We pored over garden books and planned our grand tour, each picking out her "can't miss" garden.

Arriving in London at the beginning of June, we picked up our rental car and taught ourselves how to drive on "the wrong side of the road" in the airport parking lot. We stayed in B&B's and toured gardens large and small, some on the itinerary and some that weren't. Our last stop was far off the beaten path, at Mottisfont Abbey in Hampshire. We found it by

the thing perhaps is to eat flowers
and not to be afraid

e.e. cummings

driving down a road that can only be described as a goat path that opened up into a breathtaking vista of roses. The original building at Mottisfont was a priory, founded by an advisor to King Richard the Lionhearted, King John and Henry III. Today, Mottisfont Abbey is home to the famous collection of historic shrub roses created by Graham Stuart Thomas (you might say they smelled good enough to eat, but that's getting ahead of the story).

I fall in love

Like so many other public gardens, the Abbey has places for that wonderful English tradition known as afternoon tea, which sustains you until dinnertime. Joanne and Michele opted for tea and scones; I, on the other hand, spotted a little cup of rose petal ice cream. I have to tell you that I consider ice cream one of the main building blocks of the food groups.

I put a spoonful into my mouth and discovered heaven on earth. The fragrance of the roses enveloped my tongue with perfume like nothing else I had ever eaten. I was in love. Unfortunately, there was no one around to ask for the recipe. When we came home I searched the Internet and found not only rose petal ice cream but a whole world of edible flowers and recipes. I started making some of the dishes, creating new recipes, experimenting with the endless varieties of flavors. And that is how this book came to be.

Who eats flowers?

Often, when I first mention to my guests that I cook with edible flowers, they roll their eyes at me, thinking I'm going to have them grazing on flowers. Actually, just about everyone has eaten edible flowers at some point in their lifetime. Zucchini blossoms in an Italian frittata, dandelion wine, rose petal jam and rose hip jam, broccoli, Brussels sprouts – all are examples of edible flowers and flower buds. There are the flowers of common herbs, thyme and rosemary among them, and some derivatives too, such as the seeds and seed pods of plants like sunflower seeds and the quintessential vanilla seed pod from *Vanilla planifolia*, a member of the orchid family. I was amazed to discover the extent of the edible flowers available to me.

More than just a pretty face

Not only are they used as food, some companies use them in vitamins and supplements – lutein, for example, which is in vitamin formulations for eyesight,

and is derived from marigolds *(Tagetes species)*. For a period of time there was a product on the market that was designed to "increase pleasure" for women with natural ingredients. The ingredient was *Salvia officinalis*, also known as common garden sage, a seasoning used for Thanksgiving turkey stuffing. So instead of taking a nap after dinner, you might be having other thoughts.

But this book isn't about remedies or being serious about eating only flowers. It's all about having fun with your food by taking everyday recipes and changing them into something unique – and of course to impress your friends and family too!

I wish you many happy edible adventures with the flowers in your life. Bon appétit!

RULES FOR EATING EDIBLE FLOWERS

- Eat flowers only when you are positive they are edible.
- Just because it is served with food, does not mean a flower is edible.
- DO NOT eat flowers from florists, nurseries or garden centers; they have probably been sprayed.
- Eat only from flowers that have been grown organically without pesticides.
- If you have hay fever, asthma or severe allergies, you should avoid eating members of the daisy family because they could trigger an allergic reaction.
- Children under the age of 4 should not eat edible flowers because of possible reactions.

- Remove pistils and stamens from flowers before eating. Eat only the petals.
- Do not eat flowers picked from the side of a road. Besides exhaust emissions on the plants, you don't know whose dog was there before you!
- There are many varieties of any one flower. Flowers taste different when grown in different locations.
- Introduce flowers slowly into your diet in the way you would new foods.
- Not all flowers are edible. Some are poisonous (see below).

WHAT FLOWERS ARE NOT EDIBLE?

Be aware that many innocent-looking and beautiful flowers are not to be eaten because they can cause toxic reactions and serious illness. Here is a partial list of common garden flowers that should not be consumed.

Azalea	*Rhododendron spp.*	**Iris**	*Iris versicolor and spp.*
Boxwood	*Buxus spp.*	**Ivy (English Ivy)**	*Hedera helix and spp.*
Burning Bush	*Euonymus alatus and spp.*	**Jack in the pulpit**	*Arisaema triphyllum*
Caladium	*Caladium x hortulanum*	**Lantana**	*Lantana camera*
Clematis	*Clematis spp.*	**Lily of the Valley**	*Convalaria majus*
Cosmos	*Cosmos bipinnatus and C. sulphureus*	**Lobelia**	*Lobelia erinus, L. cardinalis*
Daffodil	*Narcissus spp.*	**Morning glory**	*Ipomea purpurea and spp.*
Delphinium	*Delphinium elatum, D. consolida and spp.*	**Mountain laurel**	*Kalmia latifolia*
		Oleander	*Nerium oleander*
Elephant ears	*Colocasia esculenta*	**Periwinkle**	*Vinca major, V. minor and spp.*
Four o'clocks	*Mirabilis jalapa*		
Foxglove	*Digitalis purpurea*	**Privet**	*Ligustrum spp.*
Hyacinth	*Hyacinthus spp.*	**Rhododendron**	*Rhododendron spp.*
Hydrangea	*Hydrangea spp.*	**Sweet pea**	*Lathryus spp.*
		Wisteria	*Wisteria spp.*

GATHERING AND PREPARING EDIBLE FLOWERS

When to gather

Gather flowers (and herbs) early in the morning before the heat of the day but after the dew has dried. The essential oils are most intense in the morning and the flower petals are filled with moisture. Rinse them in cool water only if needed to remove dirt and debris. (If you are keeping the flower whole, and the top of the flower is flat enough, you can place it upside down to allow moisture to drain out.)

Proper handling

Remove petals or flowers from stems at this time. With some flower petals, like roses or tulips, you should remove the white part of the petal because it is usually very bitter. You can simply pinch it off with your fingernail or use a pair of scissors. You should also remove the stamens and pistil from the flower. That is the center part of the flower.

For fresh use

If you are going to use them fresh, place them in a plastic bag with a damp paper towel and keep them in the refrigerator until ready to use. You can prepare most flowers up to two days ahead of time. Don't over-fill the bag so as not to crush the petals.

For drying

If you are drying them for future use, allow them to dry naturally on a paper towel or a paper plate. It will take a few days for them to dry completely depending on humidity. A dark, cool, airy place works well for drying the petals. Flower petals that are thick, like roses, will take longer to dry properly than, say, bee balm. If drying a whole stem such as lavender, hanging it upside down helps it dry faster. You can also dry bundles of lavender by simply taking a rubber band and wrapping the stems several times then hanging them from a piece of string pulled across a doorway, or on a folding laundry rack. Just attach with a clothespin.

All flowers dry darker than the original color so remember that reds and purples will be dark red/purple to almost black. Yellows, oranges and pinks retain the best color. You should store your dried flowers in tightly lidded glass jars and away from light and heat since that will destroy the delicate flavors.

EDIBLE FLOWERS

ANISE HYSSOP
(Agastache foeniculum)

DESCRIPTION

Sometimes called licorice mint, this is a wonderful herb with a licorice scent, both the leaves and the flowers. The individual flowers are a bluish purple on a tall flower stem. Anise hyssop grows in most parts of the United States in full sun or partial shade. Average, well-drained soil is the ideal place for anise hyssop to thrive in the garden.

Anise Hyssop

SENSE APPEAL

The primary sense appeal is that its fragrance is close to that of anise – a mild licorice flavor, more anise than black licorice.

USES

Anise hyssop can be used as a substitution many times in a recipe. For a creamy licorice flavor in whipping cream, use the leaves and flowers instead of anise. For use in a cake recipe, use the flowers, chopped fine. The flowers are lovely candied for baked good decorations. See recipe for **Anise Hyssop Syrup** on p. 83.

BE AWARE THAT...

If you are pregnant, be sure to research possible contraindications to using this herb.

APPLE BLOSSOM
(Malus hybrid)

DESCRIPTION

An apple tree in full blossom is a joy to behold. But unless there is an apple tree growing near you, you are not likely to encounter their lovely pink and white flowers. Depending on the variety of tree and your local climate zone, blossoms (and later, apples) will appear in late spring or summer, or early fall. Before you decide to plant an apple tree of your own, check with your local extension agent to see which varieties of apples do well in your area. A good, well-drained but moist soil is ideal. Full sun is necessary for adequate flower and fruit production.

SENSE APPEAL

Apple blossoms have a faint apple/floral scent to them. The fresh beauty of a spray of apple blossoms is reason enough to bring them inside.

Apple Blossom

USES

You can float apple blossoms in punch, crystallize them or sprinkle them over a spring salad for color and a subtle floral scent.

ARTICHOKE
(Cynara scolymus)

Field of Artichokes

DESCRIPTION

These tall aliens of the garden thrive in almost all gardens. They need a pH of about 5.6 to 7.0 for a good crop. In milder climates, they can be considered a perennial vegetable. The part we eat is technically a bud. When the bud matures it opens to a purple flower, but the fully opened flower isn't considered edible because of a lack of flavor.

SENSE APPEAL

Artichokes have their own unique flavor. Nothing else tastes quite like them. As a pleasant bonus, if you have a sip of water after a bite of artichoke your mouth will experience a lovely sweet sensation.

USES

You can add a dipping sauce such as Hollandaise, clarified butter or whatever your heart desires. Whole artichokes can be stuffed with any number of tasty fillings, and their hearts can be pickled or marinated in Italian dressing. See recipe for **Artichoke Chicken Salad with Jasmine Rice** on p. 65.

4

BACHELOR BUTTON
(Centaurea cyanus)

DESCRIPTION

Also known as cornflower, bachelor button is most commonly seen as a blue flower, but there are other cultivars whose flowers are white, pink, lavender and even dark maroon. This is a very easy annual to grow. Practically pest free, these plants can be between 1 to 3 feet tall in the garden, so plant them in the back where they will provide a perfect foil for annuals and perennials, and their colorful flowers will stand up singly above the foliage.

SENSE APPEAL

Bachelor button has a light, sweet fragrance with a sweet, pleasantly spicy taste.

Bachelor Button

USES

The edible part is the beautiful petals. Add them to a salad or sprinkle on a cake.

BASIL
(Ocimum basilicum)

Basil

DESCRIPTION

Everything about basil is edible, both its leaves and its flowers. The plant's thin leaves are a medium green with the shape varying between cultivars. It is best to pinch basil once it is growing in the garden to encourage it to become bushy. The flower spike can range from white to a purplish pink color, depending on which basil you are growing. Once the flower stalk is about ¾ blooming, you can harvest the flowers. Harvest early in the day for best flavor.

SENSE APPEAL

The wonderful flavor and fragrance of basil perfumes the air whether it is used fresh or dried. While there are many types of basil, including ornamental ones, we use edible basils such as 'Genovese,' 'Sweet Large Leaf' and 'Lettuce Leaf.' Always use an edible basil (rather than an ornamental one) for the best flavor. The flowers usually have a stronger flavor than the leaves.

USES

You can include both flower and leaves in most recipes that call for basil, from soups to breads to salads – although the flower should be used in a smaller quantity due to its intense pungency.

BORAGE
(*Borago officinalis*)

Borage

DESCRIPTION

Borage is a warm season herb, so it is best to sow your seed just after the last frost. It likes to be grown in full sun with a moisture-retentive soil. Both flowers and leaves are edible. The flowers can be blue, pink or white, but most often you will see them blue.

SENSE APPEAL

The leaves have a sweet, cucumber flavor to them, making them an ideal addition to salad, and the flowers can be candied.

USES

The flavorful leaves make an ideal addition to a salad. The flowers can be candied and used on cakes or other baked goods. See recipe for **Borage Syrup** on p.83.

BE AWARE THAT...

Borage should be used in moderation. Some studies suggest that over-consumption can cause kidney problems.

BROCCOLI
(Brassica oleracea)

Broccoli

DESCRIPTION

The green part of the broccoli head is known as a floret. A yellow flower emerges from that as the floret matures. Broccoli is fairly easy to grow. It's a member of the crucifer family, such as cauliflower and Brussels sprouts. Broccoli likes cool weather and will go to seed in hot weather. You can start broccoli inside about 5 to 6 weeks before the last average frost, or outside just after the last average frost.

SENSE APPEAL

Both floret and flower are edible, with the flower having a more subtle flavor.

USES

With its crunchy texture, broccoli is ideal for Asian dishes with a little drizzle of Oriental dressing or a warm cheese sauce. See recipe for **Oriental Broccoli Salad** on p. 68.

8

EDIBLE FLOWERS

CALENDULA
(Calendula officinalis)

DESCRIPTION

Calendula is also known as pot marigold and is prized in herb gardens for attracting butterflies and for use in culinary dishes. The flowers can be orange, golden yellow, or even apricot. The plant is very easy to grow, but you should sow seed early in the spring before the last frost. It prefers full sun with a moisture-retentive soil. Cut back occasionally to encourage blooms.

SENSE APPEAL

With a slightly peppery taste, calendulas add a light, tangy flavor to breads, salads and soups – as well as color.

Calendula

USES

Calendula can be added to corn muffin and bread recipes, or used in soups and salads. It will impart color and flavor to butters and cheese sauces. You can also sprinkle it on appetizers to add a little zip of edible color. See recipes for **Calendula Butter** on p. 81, and **Calendula Corn Muffins** on p. 60.

CAULIFLOWER
(Brassica oleracea var. botrytis)

Cauliflower

DESCRIPTION

Cauliflower cultivation has the same requirements as broccoli. It belongs to the same family – crucifers. Cauliflower has newer cultivars that have red, orange and purple florets, making it even more attractive as a vegetable in the garden – or as part of a centerpiece arrangement for the table.

SENSE APPEAL

Let's face it, cauliflower has always gotten a bad rap, but roasting brings out great flavor. The new cultivars of cauliflower add color to otherwise bland dishes and awaken the curiosity of (heretofore) cauliflower naysayers.

USES

Young florets are always best for eating raw or steamed. You can serve cauliflower raw in salads or with a dip, or steamed, deep fried or stir fried. If you cook it, try sprinkling a little cheese on top and putting it under the broiler for a minute.

CHAMOMILE
(Chamaemelum nobile)

DESCRIPTION

Chamomile is a lovely little annual with yellow or white flowers. It can be used as a groundcover if they are planted close to each other. It prefers full sun and evenly moist soils to be established. In use as far back as the ancient Egyptians, chamomile has long been appreciated both for its flavor and as a folk remedy.

SENSE APPEAL

Chamomile has a scent unto itself so it's best to use it in a sweet or mainly sweet dish.

USES

It is most commonly enjoyed as a pleasantly soothing tea. Making chamomile tea and using the tea as a substitute for water in recipes gives it

Chamomile

an almost universal ingredient status. Tea breads, cookies and cakes all benefit from chamomile's flavor. If the recipe doesn't call for water, but instead uses vegetable oil, you can soak a chamomile tea bag in the oil for a few hours to get the full flavor.

BE AWARE THAT...

You should not consume chamomile if you are taking certain medications, such as blood thinners.

CHIVE
(Allium schoenoprasum)

DESCRIPTION

Chives thrive almost anywhere. You can grow them in pots or in the ground and they will reproduce early. Stems and flowers are all edible, but be sure to harvest the flowers before the plant begins to form seeds.

SENSE APPEAL

The delicate onion flavor of the stems and flowers adds a light onion taste to almost any dish.

Chive

USES

You can usually substitute the flower for the stem, no matter the dish. It will brighten up egg dishes with its onion-y flavor. It enhances potato salad and any potato recipe, for that matter. Sprinkle it over beans, or mix it into sour cream or Greek yogurt for a colorful dip. See recipe for **Chive Butter** on p. 81.

12

DANDELION
(*Taraxacum officinale*)

DESCRIPTION

Dandelions are an herbaceous perennial weed with basal leaves (growing at the base of the plant) and sunny yellow flowers, followed by white, puffy seed heads. They can be highly invasive. This is not something you find in the grocery store, but rather in the backyard. In the spring they are literally everywhere, giving you a veritable bonanza of blossoms and leaves.

SENSE APPEAL

The young flowers and buds have a sweet flavor, becoming stronger and bitter as they age.

USES

The raw leaves can be harvested for salad and the flowers (which should be cooked) can be used for a number of dishes, including stir-fry, jellies and wine. See recipes for **Dandelion Liqueur** on p. 78, and **Dandelion Syrup** on p. 83.

BE AWARE THAT . . .

The flower stem contains a milky sap and is toxic. As with all plants that you harvest, always make sure that they are growing in the soil or that they have not been treated with any pesticides.

Dandelion

DAYLILY
(Hemerocallis spp.)

Daylily

DESCRIPTION

Daylilies are one of the easiest flowers to harvest. Simply snip off the flower or the flower bud and get ready to eat it. They grow just about anywhere, in full sun or partial shade, bloom from early to late summer and come in a multitude of colors.

SENSE APPEAL

It has a vegetable-floral taste to it.

USES

You can sauté the buds or stuff the flowers with almost any filling. Just remember: the lighter the flower color, the better the taste.

EDIBLE FLOWERS

DIANTHUS
(*D. caryophyllus; D. gratianopolitanus*)

DESCRIPTION

Dianthus is a close relative of the floral favorite, carnation. They are commonly known as "pinks" although they can be red, pink, purple or even white. The edible dianthus is the one called 'Clove Pink,' and it can be either an annual or perennial. Dianthus flowers are small, about 2" across. You can grow them from seed or find plant packs in garden centers.

SENSE APPEAL

The flowers of 'Clove Pink' have a wonderful clove scent.

Dianthus

USES

Dianthus is best used in sweet dishes, but be sure to remove the bitter white ends of the flowers first. This lovely flower is great when incorporated into baked goods, like a yellow cake.

EASTERN REDBUD
(Cercis canandensis)

Eastern Redbud

DESCRIPTION

Eastern redbud is one of the beautiful native trees that flower in the spring. You will see their bright pink flowers growing along the twigs, branches and trunk. Eastern redbud grows as far west as Arkansas, north to Canada, south into northern Florida, and all through the eastern states. It is a small tree (20 to 25 feet), with multiple stems. In the wild it can be found as an understory tree, growing below the larger forest trees.

SENSE APPEAL

The bright pink flowers are crunchy with a light vegetable flavor.

USES

I like using the flowers as a topper on deviled eggs. The flowers give it a crunchy texture along with extra flavor – and make it looks so pretty, too. Eastern redbud flowers are sometimes used in game dishes, such as venison or wild boar.

ELDERBERRY
(Sambucus nigra subsp. canandensis)

DESCRIPTION

Elderberry is a medium-sized native shrub that grows over much of North America. *Sambucus canandensis* prefers a moist rich soil in full sun, but will tolerate partial shade. It is prized as a habitat/pollinator plant as well as providing wonderful and tasty purple black berries. You can use not only the familiar fruit but the elderflower as well.

SENSE APPEAL

The flavor of the berry is sweet. You can only describe the taste as "just like an elderberry." The flower has a lighter scent. *Note:* Do not wash the flowers, as this removes the flavor.

Elderberry

USES

There are many recipes for elderflower sparkling wine or cordials. The flowers are fragrant and have been used in cosmetics since antiquity. The flowers can be used to scent sparkling waters and champagnes, and they make a refreshing tea. Elderflowers can be incorporated into fruit salads. See recipe for **Elderberry Liqueur** on p. 78.

BE AWARE THAT...

Elderberries (not the flowers) must be cooked – eating them raw can cause gastric upset.

FALSE RED YUCCA
(Hesperaloe parviflora)

False Red Yucca

DESCRIPTION

The reddish pink flower of this great landscape plant is known for its reddish pink flower. False red yucca is a tough, drought tolerant plant once established. It thrives in the heat and sun of Texas, Arizona and New Mexico and likes a well draining alkaline soil. It is actually a grass, not a true yucca. Once the plant is established, it will send up flower shoots beginning in early summer, depending on location. It can also be divided once it reaches full growth.

SENSE APPEAL

The flower has a wonderful crunchy texture with the flavor a cross between a sugar snap pea and corn – or the flavor of cucumber and lettuce, depending on who's talking.

USES

It makes a wonderful addition to salads or other raw dishes. Dress it up in a salad with a little balsamic vinaigrette for a light meal.

EDIBLE FLOWERS

FENNEL
(*Foeniculum vulgare*)

DESCRIPTION

This Italian favorite vegetable utilizes the bulb as well as the flower. Although fennel is considered a perennial as far north as Zone 7, it is typically used as an annual and harvested as a vegetable. Easy to grow from seed, the only caution is not to plant it near dill since they can pollinate each other and you can end up with an odd tasting plant. The entire fennel plant can be used for cooking from the bulb to the flower and seeds.

SENSE APPEAL

The fennel flower adds the anise/licorice flavor to food without overpowering it.

Fennel

USES

Fennel's mild licorice flavor lends itself to fish, meats and other vegetables. You can mince the flower and add it to roasted asparagus or other roasted vegetables for a light fennel accent. For a wonderful luncheon dish without too much fuss, broil fish with fennel flowers.

GARLIC, GARLIC SCAPE
(Allium sativum)

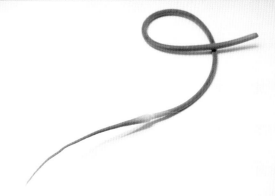

Garlic Scape

DESCRIPTION

Garlic needs little introduction. If you wish to grow it, garlic should be planted in the fall for harvest the next spring. It is harvested when the foliage dies down. Less well known is the garlic scape, which is the immature flower head of garlic – the long, green, curly part. It is usually harvested once it appears, in order to allow all the plant's energy to go to the garlic bulb.

SENSE APPEAL

While the garlic scape isn't truly a flower, it is part two of a "twofer." Not only is the bulb of garlic delicious but the scape provides a slightly milder flavor version of garlic.

USES

The scapes are often used as a substitute for basil in pesto recipes. They are great simply sautéed in some olive oil and butter and tossed with pasta with some good grated cheese. Scapes are sometimes substituted for asparagus.

GERANIUM (Lime & Rose)
(Pelargonium nervosum & P. graveolens)

DESCRIPTION

Lime and rose geranium are two favorites from the large group of aromatic, flavorful geraniums. Easily grown as houseplants or outdoors, their leaves actually provide more of the flavor than the flowers, but there are plenty of uses for both. The lime geranium's leaves are very small, the rose geranium's are larger and are velvety to the touch.

SENSE APPEAL

Lime geranium's leaves have quite a strong lime-citrus flavor – the flowers less so. The flowers and leaves of rose geranium have the scent of roses, but not their sweetness; yet they have a special place in the flavor palette.

Rose Geranium

USES

Harvest them and mince them fine if using in a dish or leave them whole if you are making a jelly with the leaves. Since the leaves can be tough, they can be bruised and added to liquid ingredients in recipes such as oils, vinegars and cream (strain after a few hours and use as directed in the recipe). Rose geranium leaves can be used to add scent to baked goods by layering them on the bottom of a baking pan. The flowers of both types can be added to fruit punches or candied as a colorful topper for desserts…and then eaten!

HERBES DE PROVENCE

Herbes de Provence

DESCRIPTION

Herbes de Provence isn't a single flower, but a blend of typical French and Italian herbs from the Provence region of France, many of them flowering herbs. The blend usually contains rosemary, lavender, basil, thyme, marjoram, bay leaf, chervil, sage, savory, fennel, oregano and tarragon, although it can vary. The key is freshness.

SENSE APPEAL

It imparts a wonderful combination of savory but floral accents to most dishes.

USES

It should be added while cooking, and it is especially taste-enhancing in poultry dishes. See recipe for **Chicken Herbes de Provence** on p. 71.

HIBISCUS
(H. syriacus, H. rosa-sinensus, H. sabdariffa)

DESCRIPTION

A few varieties of hibiscus are edible: the ubiquitous Rose of Sharon, H. syriacus, found in way too many landscapes, the luscious tropical hibiscus, H. rosa-sinensus, and the poor sister of the group, Roselle, H. sabdariffa – all are edible and used in various ways.

SENSE APPEAL

The flavor of the flowers is mildly sweet or citrusy or slightly nutty, depending on the variety.

USES

The petals are commonly used for herbal teas, hot or iced. In Jamaica, Roselle's petals are used for making a sweet drink mixed with cane sugar and herbs and served at Christmas time. When hibiscus petals are mixed with carbonated water

"Brilliant" Hibiscus

or lemon lime drink, the result is very refreshing. The Rose of Sharon flowers and the tropical hibiscus flowers can also be torn and tossed into salads that have some fruit in them, since the flowers are slightly sweet. See recipe for **Hibiscus Liqueur on p. 78.**

BE AWARE THAT...

Roselle can also act as a diuretic, so it should be taken in small doses.

LAVENDER
(Lavandula angustifolia)

Lavender

DESCRIPTION

Lavender is a small, extremely fragrant, evergreen shrub that likes a fertile, well-drained soil in full sun. The flowers are edible and small quantities of the leaves as well. You can find it dried in the herb section or fresh at farmers markets.

SENSE APPEAL

Of the many species of lavender, angustifolia, or English lavender, is the one most often used in cooking. It imparts a sweet, subtle quality to a wide variety of foods.

USES

What can't you use lavender for in the kitchen? You can make wonderful vinegar with it for salad, put it in baked goods, use the stems to smoke pork on a grill, make lemonade or let your imagination run wild. See recipes for **Caramelized Onions with Lavender** on p. 59, **Lavender Syrup** on p. 84, **Strawberry Lavender Delight** on p. 76, **Malibu Margaritas** on p. 79.

BE AWARE THAT...

Dried lavender buds that are used for sachets are often treated with oils to preserve the scent. Make sure you buy culinary lavender only.

LEMON BALM
(Melissa officinalis)

DESCRIPTION

Lemon balm is a very easy to grow herb in full sun. It can be invasive, so it is best grown in a container to keep it in check. It blooms in late summer and its flowers are small and creamy colored. Bees love them, so take care as you collect your blossoms.

SENSE APPEAL

Its lemony herbal flavor in both flowers and leaves allows it to be used in a number of dishes.

USES

It can be used in vinegars, combined chopped with other herbs for a garni in cooking – or you can simply take a handful of leaves and flowers and stuff them into the cavity of poultry, and allow the flavor to permeate while cooking. See recipe for **Lemon Balm Syrup** on p. 83.

Lemon Balm

LEMON VERBENA
(Aloysia triphylla)

Lemon Verbena

DESCRIPTION

Lemon verbena is a woody shrub that thrives in most parts of the country in full sun. It can be grown in a container in an area where it is not winter hardy. As with most herbs, it should be grown in average moist soil in full sun. The tiny creamy white flowers should be harvested as soon they open. The narrow green leaves should be stripped off the stem for use. They can be dried, but the best flavor is when it is used fresh.

SENSE APPEAL

Lemon verbena has a bright, tangy lemon flavor.

USES

Its bright lemon flavor allows it to be used in jellies, jams, desserts, teas, scenting syrups and cream. Both the flowers and leaves impart a delightful flavor to poultry and seafood dishes. See recipe for **Lemon Verbena Salmon** on p. 69.

26

LILAC
(Syringa vulgaris)

DESCRIPTION

The common lilac is an old fashioned shrub. It prefers full sun and good air flow for optimum growth. The flowers can be pink, purple, reddish purple and white. The best lilacs for eating are the ones with the most fragrance. The flowers should be harvested before all the buds are open, early in the morning. Pick off the individual flowers one by one.

SENSE APPEAL

Lilac is, well... lilac. Its heavenly fragrance has made it a favorite for not only bouquets but perfumes as well. What is little known is that the lilac flower is edible and delicious.

Lilac

USES

Since the flowers are fleshy, they are best used fresh. Mix them with a little cream cheese and spread on a sandwich or cracker, or stir into yogurt. Try making a simple syrup from the flowers and pouring it over crepes or fruit. **Tip:** when using lilac flowers in a syrup, add a few blueberries for color since the lilacs cook to an unappetizing greenish color. See recipe for **Lilac Syrup** on p. 83.

SIGNET MARIGOLD
(Tagetes tenufolia)

Signet Marigold

DESCRIPTION

Tagetes is a genus of 56 marigold species. It grows all over North America and is a favorite in gardens for its color and sometimes as a garden bug repellent. Signet marigold does that and more: it tastes good. Signet is a small marigold with single petals and ferny, citrus-scented foliage. The best signet varieties for using in foods are 'Lemon Gem' and 'Orange Gem.'

SENSE APPEAL

The flowers have a vegetable/lemon flavor to them. Nice and citrusy.

USES

The petals can be added to cold dishes or incorporated into soups or cheese dishes. See recipe for **Marigold Tofu "Eggless" Egg Salad** on p. 67.

EDIBLE FLOWERS

MARJORAM
(Origanum marjorana)

DESCRIPTION

Often confused with oregano, marjoram is a Mediterranean herb. The leaves are used in Greek and Italian dishes, but the small, white flowers are edible as well. Marjoram is easy to grow as a potted plant on a sunny porch or in a bright kitchen window. It's always best to use the fresh herb in cooking, if possible.

SENSE APPEAL

The leaves have a citrus-pine flavor. The flavor of the flowers is milder.

Marjoram

USES

Marjoram flowers and leaves match well with poultry, fish, lamb, soups and stuffings. A note about the flowers: to be sure that the delicate flavor of the flowers is preserved, they are best harvested as they open, and tossed into dishes that don't require cooking, or at the end of cooking.

MINT
(Mentha spp.)

Mint

DESCRIPTION

The mint family is extensive, including sage, marjoram, rosemary, oregano, catnip – and the mintiest members, which include spearmint, peppermint, apple mint, chocolate… and many more. One of the distinguishing characteristics is the square stem. Mint is almost always a perennial and can be invasive if left unchecked. It is best to grow mint in a pot or a bed that is contained.

SENSE APPEAL

The mint family offers a bouquet of refreshing scents and flavors that are almost ubiquitous in our lives – from toothpaste to shampoo to, well, mints.

USES

Mint lends itself to sweeter dishes, like candies and baked goods, not to mention the favorite Southern Mint Julep. The flowers are just as potent as the leaves, so add a little and taste before using too much. See recipes for **Watermelon and Feta Salad** on p. 66, and **Mint Liqueur** on p. 78.

EDIBLE FLOWERS

MONARDA (BEE BALM)
(Monarda didyma)

DESCRIPTION

Bee balm is one of the newcomers to herbal history. Sometimes called wild bergamot, it is a native of North America and is one of the most prized plants in a pollinator garden. It attracts butterflies, bees and hummingbirds. *M. didyma's* flowers can be red or purple. Harvest the flowers when they are ¾ of the way open. The entire plant is edible.

SENSE APPEAL

The fragrant flowers have a sweet, spicy citrus scent and taste to them.

Monarda (Bee Balm)

USES

Bee balm makes a wonderful addition to ice tea and lemonades, or add it to fresh fruits like pineapple or melons for accent. See recipes for **Monarda Butter** on p. 81, and **Monarda Syrup** on p. 83.

See recipes for **Monarda Butter** on p. 81, and **Monarda Syrup** on p. 83.

NASTURTIUM
(Tropaeolum majus)

Nasturtium

DESCRIPTION

Nasturtiums are considered an annual in most areas. This brightly colored flower loves full summer sun and below average soil fertility. They are easily started from seed and there are several cultivars, including 'Alaska,' 'Jewel,' and 'Whirlybird.' The flowers range from yellow to reds and orange, with leaves that can be solid green or variegated. Some are climbers while others are bushy. The flowers, the leaves and seed pods are all edible. You can sometimes find them in the grocery store in the fresh herb section where they sell packaged herbs and flowers, or at a farmers market.

SENSE APPEAL

The leaves and flowers have a peppery flavor to them and the seed pods can be pickled and used in place of capers.

USES

Nasturtiums are wonderful used in salads, soups, stuffed as an appetizer, a garnish or to punch up an otherwise bland dish. See recipes for **Fresh Salsa with Pineapple and Nasturtiums** on p. 57, **Nasturtium Bundles** on p. 63, **Asian Noodles Vinaigrette with Nasturtiums** on p. 72, **Salmon Pizza with Nasturtiums** on p. 70.

ONION FLOWER
(Allium cepa)

Onion Flower

DESCRIPTION

Onions are one of the most popular vegetables used in cooking. They can be red, white or yellow, with varying degrees of sweetness or pungency. Onions can be grown throughout the Northern Hemisphere. You can grow onions from either seed or what is referred to as "sets" of small bulbils. While we are used to cooking with the bulb or the leaves, many forget about the flower which offers an onion flavor without the bite of onion. Just leave a few onion bulbs in the ground and it will send up a flower stalk topped with a round white flower similar to the ornamental alliums. Harvest as soon as the flowers open.

SENSE APPEAL

Onion flavors can range from sweet to pungent.

USES

Onion is such an ancient plant that it has had time to become a basic ingredient in almost every culture's cuisine. It can be tossed in a salad, mixed with vegetables, either raw or cooked, fresh or dried. Onion flowers provide their own accent to what could be an otherwise bland dish. See recipe for **Oven Roasted Italian Green Beans with Onion Flowers** on p. 61.

ORANGE BLOSSOM
(Citrus sinensis)

Orange Blossom

DESCRIPTION

Also known as the sweet orange, *Citrus sinensis* is a tropical tree that grows in the warmer regions of North America, and as a house plant in the northern states. Many beekeepers place their hives in orange groves, allowing the bees to produce orange blossom honey.

SENSE APPEAL

The flavor of orange blossoms is mild compared to the fruit, but the blossoms offer something extra: their delightful fragrance, as anyone knows who has ever been near an orange tree or grove in bloom.

USES

Because of their fragrance, the blossoms are useful as a garnish in fruit salads or as a topping over roasted asparagus. The blossoms can also be candied or used in teas and lemonades. See recipe for **Orange Blossom Liqueur** on p. 78.

34

OREGANO
(*Origanum vulgare* subsp. *hirtum*)

DESCRIPTION

Oregano is an herb commonly used in Greek, Italian and Mexican cuisine. Another member of the mint family, it is a perennial that readily reseeds itself, so place it in an area where it won't become a pest. Both leaves and flowers are edible. The small, pinkish purple flowers can be dried for storage or used fresh.

SENSE APPEAL

Oregano has a warm and almost balsamic taste, making it desirable for use in a variety of dishes.

USES

When using fresh oregano flowers, a little goes a long way. Add as desired for strength. It is wonderful in tomato dishes, on pizzas and in fresh

Oregano

bread – or mixed with a little butter and spread onto crostini for an appetizer. See recipe for **Oregano Butter** on p. 81.

EDIBLE FLOWERS

PANSY
(Viola x wittrockiana)

Pansy

DESCRIPTION

Pansies are one of the most beloved spring flowers, with a palette of colors when not much else is blooming. They are a cool weather annual that is happy in either the spring or fall in most parts of North America. They have a larger flower than the similar-looking viola.

SENSE APPEAL

The flowers are slightly sweet.

USES

Pansy flowers can be candied and used in desserts, added to butter and cream cheese for a tea sandwich filling, or tossed in a fresh salad. For some party pizzazz, freeze some flowers in an ice ring for punch. See recipe for **Pansy Syrup** on p. 85.

PASSIONFLOWER
(*Passiflora vitifolia*)

DESCRIPTION

There are more than 500 species of passionflower around the world, in various colors of blue, purple, yellow and, in the case of *Passiflora vitifolia*, bright red. Also known as the Crimson Passionflower, this edible floral is native to the temperate regions of the Americas and produces an edible flower. It is a beautiful vine, hardy in the southern United States, but doesn't do well in areas of hard frost. Another cultivar, *Passiflora edulis*, has a delicious fruit, but its flower is not very tasty. It's good to know the difference.

SENSE APPEAL

The flower is slightly sweet.

Passionflower

USES

Since the flower blooms just one at a time, it is difficult to grow a usable crop from just one plant. Where it grows wild, it is made into jams and jellies. Thinning it with a little warmed apple juice makes it an ideal flavoring for a jasmine rice salad.

GARDEN PEA
(Pisum sativum)

Garden Pea

DESCRIPTION

Peas are one of the earliest spring crops, twining their way up a trellis in the garden. They prefer cool weather for germination and growth. Everyone knows about peas in the pod, but it's time to give the flowers their due. The mild crunchiness and flavor of the pea flower allows it to be one of those delicious moments in the garden when you can literally pick and eat the flower at the peak of perfection. Of course, don't eat all the flowers if you want actual peas later on! The familiar snow pea (shown in the photo at right) is another type of garden pea.

SENSE APPEAL

Pea flowers have a light vegetable fresh pea taste to them, with a satisfying crunch as well.

USES

Since the pea flower flavor is so delicate, it is best used as a garnish or tossed into a salad or on a raw vegetable platter.

BE AWARE THAT...

The garden pea is **not** the same as the fragrant **sweet pea**. Sweet pea *(Lathyrus odoratus)* is not an edible plant and can be toxic.

38

PINEAPPLE GUAVA
(Acca sellowiana syn. Feijoa sellowiana)

DESCRIPTION

This wonderful evergreen shrub produces not only a wonderful fruit but a delicious and beautiful flower as well, with exquisite pale pink, slightly fleshy petals. Pineapple guava is well suited to growing in mild coastal areas such as California. An easy to grow shrub with few pests, it only requires some shelter from wind in a windy site. Many birds, robins and starlings among them, like the petals, so you may have some competition.

SENSE APPEAL

The flower petals have a flavor that has been described as cotton candy with guava overtones. Pineapple guava's fruit is similar in flavor to apple guava, the most common of the many guava species.

Pineapple Guava

USES

The pulp of the fruit has been used in chutneys, in fruit salads and eaten out of hand. The guava-cotton candy flavor of the petals makes them ideal for incorporating into a fruit salad, sugared, or added to a smoothie or milkshake. See recipe for **Pineapple Guava Smoothie** on p. 80.

PINEAPPLE SAGE
(Salvia elegans)

Pineapple Sage

DESCRIPTION

Pineapple sage is a kissing cousin of the mint family. Its botanical name, *Salvia elegans*, describes the plant perfectly: an easy care salvia that is elegant, from the bright green leaves to the bright red flower. Hummingbirds love this plant, which blooms mid- to late summer in the garden. It will grow from 12 to 30 inches high and do just as well in a pot as in the garden, as long as it receives adequate water.

SENSE APPEAL

No surprise, pineapple sage has a pineapple mint flavor, slightly fruity and spicy at the same time.

USES

Both flowers and leaves are edible. Add to Middle Eastern dishes, or to seafood for a Pacific Rim taste – or tear the flowers and leaves apart and toss with fruit, especially cantaloupe. See recipe for **Sunny Shrimp** on p. 73.

PRICKLY PEAR
(*Opuntia spp.*)

DESCRIPTION

Almost all members of the *Opuntia* species (a large genus of cacti) are edible, but the ones you see in stores are *Opuntia ficus*, a long-domesticated crop plant. The flower is edible, but hard and small, so rather than harvest it, we use the pads that are formed from the blossom. Their growing range is from the southern parts of the United States as far north as Michigan. It is extremely popular in Mexican cooking, where the pads are known as *nopales*. You can find *nopales* fresh in Mexican markets or farmers markets, or canned or pickled in many supermarkets.

SENSE APPEAL

It is rather neutral in flavor, but has a pleasant texture and is a good source of vitamins and fiber.

Prickly Pear

USES

Since the prickly pear pads are on the bland side, they are a good foil for cheeses, deep frying or making pickles. They can be a delicious addition chopped into egg dishes.

RADISH
(Raphanus sativus)

Radish

DESCRIPTION

The radish grows almost anywhere in North America during the spring and the fall. Its rapid growth rate allows several sowings of seed to keep it producing. The radish flower is a small, white, singular flower that grows when the plant is left to go to seed.

SENSE APPEAL

The radish flower is a milder version of the spicy, mildly hot root vegetable.

USES

Since the flower is small, the best use is to add it to salads as a topper. It's one of those unexpected garnishes that will make people think you're a very creative cook!

ROSE
(Rosa spp.)

DESCRIPTION

Roses are what make writers write poetry, what men use as peace offerings, and what give our senses a heady perfume, and all from a thorny bush! Roses grow on at least four continents, spanning all types of growing conditions. They prefer an open, sunny site with at least six hours of direct sun. Roses grow in a rich humus soil that is moist and well drained. The best roses to use in cooking are the ones that are the most fragrant. Not only does the flower provide us with fragrance but a taste treat as well. And after the flowers have faded, they produce a fruit known as rose hip. You can find organic roses at some grocers and farmers markets or you can grow your own at home. You can also purchase dried rose petals and rose hips from herbal shops.

David Austin's 'Graham Thomas' English shrub rose

SENSE APPEAL

For culinary use it's hard to recommend only one particular rose type. I suggest Damask, Gallica and English shrub roses because most of these have wonderful fragrance, which can be sweet, cinnamon-clove, fruity and more. I myself grow 'Don Juan,' a climber with blood red petals and a delicious fragrance, but check to see which ones do well in your area.

ROSE

'Don Juan'

USES

Rose petals can be used fresh or dried, with the bitter white part of the petal removed. Chopped fresh rose petals can be added to butters, sugar, candy, baked goods, jams and preserves, fruit salad – and the list goes on. Dried rose petals can be used in many of the same ways. Of course my favorite is adding them to ice cream for the ultimate dessert. Rose hips are filled with Vitamin C and make a wonderful jam. You can also purchase seedless rose hips and reconstitute them with a little apple juice and use them in place of raisins in recipes. See recipes for **Rose Petal Jam** on p. 58, **Chocolate Pavlova with Strawberries and Rosewater** on p. 74, **Rose Petal Ice Cream** on p. 77.

EDIBLE FLOWERS

ROSEMARY
(Rosemarinus)

DESCRIPTION

Rosemary is for remembrance, as Shakespeare wrote, and once you plant it, you will always remember to have it in your garden. It is an evergreen shrub in warmer climates and an annual herb or houseplant elsewhere. The flowers can be anywhere from a bluish white to a light blue. The flowers should be used immediately after picking.

SENSE APPEAL

Brushing your hand over the bush releases a wonderful pine-citrus scent.

USES

Its use is boundless. Rosemary flowers and leaves can be used on poultry, but are especially wonderful with pork. You can snip them and add

to biscuit dough, or make an orange rosemary salad dressing. For an unforgettable barbecue, cut branches of rosemary, soak them in water and use them to smoke meats on the grill.

Rosemary

GARDEN SAGE
(Salvia officinalis)

Garden Sage

DESCRIPTION

This semi-woody herb is a perennial staple in herb gardens and Western cuisines. The gray-green leaves of this small, perennial evergreen shrub are somewhat velvety, with bluish purple flowers. Other varieties of garden sage have variegated leaves. There are about 1000 species of sage, a plant that thrives in the Mediterannean and other dry climates.

SENSE APPEAL

Sage leaves have a peppery flavor to them and can be used either fresh or dried. The flowers are milder and should be used fresh.

USES

Sage is typically used with poultry but can be used for wild game and stuffing. It also goes well as part of a simple snack of sliced hard cheese, tomato and maybe a splash of lemon and olive oil – a Mediterranean natural.

EDIBLE FLOWERS

SCARLET RUNNER BEAN
(Phaseolus coccineus)

DESCRIPTION

This plant is mainly grown in North America for its beautiful red flower, although the pods are edible when cooked. It is considered an edible ornamental, for both the flower and the vegetable.

SENSE APPEAL

There is a mild bean flavor to the flower (no surprise!).

USES

The flower is crunchy, decorative and red, ideal for use raw in salads. It can be added to bean dishes after they have been cooked. The flavor disappears from the flower when it is cooked, so be sure to wait until the last minute with these.

Scarlet Runner Bean

SQUASH FLOWER
(Cucurbita pepo)

Squash Flower

DESCRIPTION

The squash flower has long been used in cooking. While the male and female flowers are both edible, the male flower is usually the one used in cooking because of its larger size. The blossoms are harvested while they have developed but not opened. The trick is to visit your squash patch frequently, because squash grow so quickly that they move from flower stage to giant squash before you know it.

SENSE APPEAL

The flowers have a slight vegetable flavor, but they are more a beautiful golden-colored container for fillings.

USES

Squash flowers can be stuffed with cheeses and other fillings, battered and deep fried or sautéed and added to pasta.

EDIBLE FLOWERS

STRAWBERRY
(Fragaria x ananas)

DESCRIPTION

If you have ever grown strawberries in your own garden, you've seen the snowy white flowers blooming among the green leaves. While everyone knows about the mouth-watering taste of fresh strawberries, a few creative cooks have found ways to bring the small strawberry flowers into their cuisine. Strawberries can be grown in the ground or in containers.

SENSE APPEAL

The flowers retain the strawberry fragrance, as well as a milder strawberry flavor.

Strawberry

USES

Float the petals in drinks, or candy the petals for desserts. You can also add the flowers to salads. You can also add the flowers to syrups, then strain out and use as a base for lemonades. The leaves can be made into a tea.

SUNFLOWER
(Helianthus annuus)

Sunflowers

DESCRIPTION

The sunflower's sunny disposition always makes people smile. The old-fashioned flower is native to the Americas and can grow to be quite tall, 5 to 12 feet or more – so if possible, grow one of the shorter varieties so you can reach the flower. The familiar sunflower seeds result from the maturing of the inner spirals of florets of the flower head.

SENSE APPEAL

The flower petals are slightly bitter. Blanching for a few moments reduces any bitterness. Be sure to remove the white at the bottom of the petals. The flavor of the sunflower seed is mildly nutty.

USES

The flower petals can be used as a garnish and the seeds can be toasted and added to dishes, eaten raw, or enjoyed as a nut butter or a cooking oil. See recipe for **Oriental Broccoli Salad** on p. 68.

THYME
(*Thymus vulgaris*)

DESCRIPTION

Thyme is an easy to grow herb that thrives in hot sun and a well-drained moist soil. We hear most often about the thyme leaf, but the flower deserves its day in the sun. Thyme flowers are very tiny and usually white. If thyme is grown where it is hot and dry, the oils will be more concentrated in the leaves and the flavor more intense.

SENSE APPEAL

The fragrance and flavor of the thyme leaf is reminiscent of sage, but has a minty warmth to it, and a fresher taste. The flower is a slightly milder version of the leaf. Another member of the thyme family, *Thymus citriodorus*, or lemon thyme, has a slightly citrus flavor.

Thyme

USES

It can be used in flavoring butters, and also makes a wonderful vinegar. The whole stems with flowers can be stuffed inside poultry or snipped for use on foccacia or other breads. See recipes for **Thyme Butter** on p. 81, and **Mushrooms Stuffed with Fresh Mozzarella and Thyme** on p. 62.

TULIP
(Tulipa spp.)

Tulip

DESCRIPTION

Tulip flowers are one of the harbingers of spring, with their vast array of colors and sizes. Some newer varieties of tulips are even fragrant, and all are edible. They grow best in areas with long, cool springs and cold temperatures in the winter.

SENSE APPEAL

The colors of the tulips can dictate the flavor: lighter-colored flowers are always best, with a slightly sweet taste. The texture is pleasantly crisp and crunchy.

USES

Tulip flowers are mainly used as a stuffing container to hold dishes such as chicken salad or lemon curd.

VIOLA
(Viola odorata)

DESCRIPTION

Sometimes referred to as "heartsease," violas were once thought to relieve love pains of the heart. You may have heard of them referred to as "sweet violas." They are really smaller versions of pansies with the same growing conditions. The plant is generally perennial, blooming most of the spring and into summer, although some are also annuals.

SENSE APPEAL

Violas are just as sweet as pansies, with a slight fragrance.

Viola

USES

Violas, as with pansies, can be candied and used in desserts. Their sweet flavor enhances butters and soft, creamy cheeses — bringing a fresh new flavor to sandwich fillings. The flowers make a colorful splash in salad.

YUCCA
(Yucca filimentosa)

DESCRIPTION

Depending on where you live, this plant is known as Spanish sword plant (because of the sharp point on the long leaves), or simply as yucca. The creamy white, edible flowers appear on a flower spike in the middle of the plant. The leaves are used in floral arrangements and are inedible.

SENSE APPEAL

The yucca flower has a taste similar to a snow pea. Some call it a cucumber-artichoke flavor.

USES

The flower can be sautéed, boiled, added to soups and stew or stuffed with cheese.

Yucca

BE AWARE THAT...

Eating the raw flower can cause mild stomach upset. The flower should always be cooked.

54

RECIPES

Edible Flower Cream Cheese Spread

This is one of my favorite spreads. I like to make up a batch with buttery crackers for a trip. Of course it never lasts the entire trip because someone always wants more. On the sweet side, it has a spicy undertone from the Monarda and mint but the sweetness of the pansies and roses. I always have a jar of this in the house.

1 8-ounce package cream cheese, softened
1 stick butter, softened (optional)*
1 tablespoon Edible Flower mixture**
Fresh Flowers

In a mixing bowl combine cream cheese, butter and flower mixture with a mixer. Line a mold with plastic wrap then line with edible fresh flowers and add cheese spread. Wrap tightly and refrigerate for 6 hours or overnight to let flavor fully develop. Unmold and peel off plastic wrap.

Serve with plain butter crackers or cookies.

* You don't have to include butter but it gives it a smoother taste.
**Available from www.VillageHerbShop.com. Or you could use combinations of the following, being careful to adjust for flavor so that no single one is predominant: Spearmint, pansies, monarda (bee balm), roses, dianthus, calendula, marigold, nasturtium...and a little lavender (be careful – it's strong).

Fresh Salsa with Pineapple and Nasturtiums

This is one of those recipes that's referred to as "sweet with heat." It's not too hot but just tangy enough. Over beef, chicken or fish, the salsa make a great topping – or just have fun with chips and margaritas.

4 – 6 large fresh tomatoes, peeled, chopped and seeded
4 Jalapeno or Serrano peppers, tops removed, chopped and seeded
(If you like, you can add a mixture of peppers)
1 small red onion, finely chopped
1 red pepper, chopped and seeded
2 cloves garlic, finely minced
1 small can crushed pineapple, very well drained
(Press out moisture if necessary)
15 Nasturtium leaves/flowers, washed and chopped
1½ tablespoons bottled lime juice

You can make this up several hours before, to let the flavors blend together.

Combine tomatoes, peppers, onion, garlic, pineapple and nasturtiums in a bowl. Toss with lime juice and salt and pepper. Make sure tomatoes are well drained. Chill until serving. Serve with tortilla chips and sour cream, or as a topping for meats and poultry.

Makes 2½ – 3 cups

Rose Petal Jam

This delicately pink colored jam is best made with fragrant red or pink flowers for good color. Perfect to serve with tea crackers or to put on a warm croissant for a winter treat.

½ pound dark red, red or dark pink rose petals
2 cups granulated sugar
4 ½ cups water
½ cup lemon juice

Remove the bitter white bases from rose petals, then rinse petals and drain completely.

Place in a glass or stainless steel bowl. Lightly sprinkle a small amount of sugar over the petals, covering them thoroughly. Cover with plastic wrap and let sit overnight.

Place remaining sugar, water, and lemon juice in a saucepan over low heat, stirring until sugar is dissolved. Stir in rose petals and let simmer about 20 minutes. Increase heat to medium-high and bring to a rolling boil. Continue boiling for approximately 5 minutes until mixture thickens and the temperature on a candy thermometer is 220° F.

Remove from heat and place in jelly jars and process in a hot water bath.

Caramelized Onions with Lavender

I consider onions a major food group, so combining it with lavender seemed like the most natural thing in the world. The caramelized onions with the lavender create a flavorful combo that can be used as a side dish or over fish or poultry.

4 tablespoons butter
2 medium to large sweet white onions, sliced thinly
2 stems fresh lavender
or
1 tablespoon ground lavender (pulverized in a coffee or spice grinder)
1 tablespoon sugar

Melt butter in a large heavy bottomed pan or an enameled Dutch oven over low heat.

If using fresh lavender add to butter and toss to coat. If using ground lavender this will be added later.

Let the lavender sauté in the butter until very fragrant and the leaves are completely wilted. Remove from butter. Add onions and sugar. Toss to coat completely. If using dried lavender, sprinkle the lavender and sugar over the onions and toss them in the melted butter.

Stir occasionally, making sure onions are not sticking to the bottom of the pan. As they cook, the onions will become translucent and start to turn to a rich honey brown. Once they reach that stage, you can remove the pan from heat and allow the onions to cool. You can store the onions in the refrigerator for up to a week.

Use as a topping on bruschetta, over chicken or fish, or toss with pasta.

Calendula Corn Muffins

These easy muffins have calendula petals scattered throughout, giving them a tang counteracted by the sweetness of the corn. If you can use fresh-off-the-cob corn, it makes the muffins a little creamier. Sweet and tangy – perfect with chili or Sunday ham.

1 cup all-purpose flour
1 cup white cornmeal (stone ground, if possible)
½ teaspoon salt
2 teaspoons baking powder
½ teaspoon baking soda
¼ cup sugar
1 large egg

4 tablespoons butter, melted and cooled
8 ounces sour cream
½ cup milk
1 cup corn kernels, fresh or frozen
½ cup fresh calendula petals,
    white base removed

Preheat oven to 375° F.

Grease and flour 12 muffin cups, or line with paper liners. In a mixing bowl, combine the cornmeal, flour, salt, baking powder, soda and sugar. In a small bowl, whisk together the egg, sour cream, milk and melted butter; stir this into the first mixture just until blended. Stir in corn and fresh calendula petals.

Fill prepared muffin cups about 3/4 full. Bake for 20 – 25 minutes, or until lightly browned.

Serves 6 (2 muffins each)

APPETIZERS & SIDE DISHES

Oven Roasted Italian Green Beans with Onion Flowers

My mother loved green beans and she created this recipe remembering how her father made them when she was a child. My additions to this recipe are the onion flowers, which give it another flavor note. Her favorite beans for this recipe were the French green beans but any green bean will do.

½ pound fresh green beans, trimmed
2 cups water
3 tablespoon butter
¼ cup olive oil
1 tablespoon minced garlic
¼ cup pine nuts
1 tablespoon onion flowers, fresh or dried
2 tablespoons bread crumbs
¼ cup Parmesan cheese, grated

In a saucepan, bring water to a boil and cook the beans for 10 minutes. Drain and set aside.

Melt butter and oil together and add garlic. Add pine nuts, breadcrumbs and cheese. Toss with the cooked beans, place on a cookie sheet and bake at 375° F for 15 – 20 minutes or until beans are still a bit crispy but done.

Serves 2 – 3

Mushrooms Stuffed with Fresh Mozzarella and Thyme

The thyme livens up the mozzarella and highlights the flavor of the mushroom. Thyme and thyme flowers are so often overlooked, taking a back seat to the more prominent basils and rosemary. It's a fresh flavor with just a slight hint of mintiness without the sweetness, and it can be used in almost any dish, even apple pie!

¼ cup balsamic vinegar
¼ cup extra virgin olive oil
1 dozen mushrooms for stuffing, cleaned
    and stemmed
fresh mozzarella balls
1 small jar of roasted red peppers
Sprigs of fresh thyme with flowers if
    possible, picked off stem

Combine vinegar and oil and brush over mushrooms. Place mushroom caps stem side up on a baking pan. Cut small pieces of mozzarella and place in mushrooms. Top with a small piece of roasted red pepper and a few thyme leaves and flowers. Bake at 375° F until cheese melts and mushrooms are done. About 20 – 25 minutes.

Serves 4 – 6.

APPETIZERS & SIDE DISHES

Nasturtium Bundles

My friend Lyn and I were looking at our bowl of nasturtium leaves one day and were trying to figure out something different and fun to do with them. We tossed ideas back and forth as we so often do. I wanted to make a sandwich with two leaves and Lyn thought they would look attractive if they were rolled into a bundle and tied with chive stems. So to Lyn I say Thank you for these little works of art!

25 whole nasturtium leaves (more or less), freshly washed and dried
25 whole nasturtium flowers, freshly washed and dried
1 cup freshly washed and dried nasturtiums flowers and leaves, chopped
¼ cup chopped sun dried tomatoes in oil, drained and patted dry
½ pound chevre (mild goat's cheese)
½ cup chopped pine nuts
3 tablespoons chopped lime basil
25 chive stems
Salt and pepper

You need one leaf and chive stem per rollup.

In a bowl, combine cheese, chopped flowers, nuts, basil and tomatoes. Salt and pepper to taste. Place 1 teaspoon of the mixture onto back of a prepared nasturtium leaf. Roll up and secure with chive stem. Decorate your serving dish with the whole nasturtium flowers.

Makes 25 rollups (more or less)

Roasted Red Pepper Soup with Nasturtiums and Fresh Thyme

The roasted red peppers with their earthy sweet flavor are a natural companion to nasturtiums. The sour cream can tame the peppery fire and the vodka can light a fire under you.

6 large red bell peppers, roasted, seeded and cooled
or
1 16-ounce jar roasted red peppers in <u>water</u>, drained
1 32-ounce can or bottle tomato juice
2½ tomato juice cans (32-ounce) of water, chicken or
     vegetable broth (or any combination of the three)
About 1 packed cup of flowers and leaves from
     washed nasturtiums, patted dry
1 tablespoon lemon juice
Leaves from 2 sprigs of fresh thyme
     (about 4 or 5 inches long)
Salt and freshly ground pepper
Sour cream

In a food processor, puree peppers until smooth. Place in saucepan along with broth/water, tomato juice and lemon juice and heat thoroughly. Mince nasturtiums and add to soup with thyme. Add a small amount of salt and freshly ground pepper. Cook for another 5 minutes to allow flavors to meld together.

Serve hot or cold with a dollop of sour cream. This is absolutely fabulous served cold.

You can also skip the sour cream and add a tablespoon of vodka if serving cold, stirring it in. (My husband's idea.)

Makes 10 – 12 generous servings

Artichoke Chicken Salad with Jasmine Rice

We like the flavors in this salad because they are so diverse but come together so well. The Chinese sweet chili sauce is offset by the creamy coolness of the coconut milk, and the jasmine rice is a wonderful base for the ingredients. Where's the flower? Why, the artichoke, of course!

4 whole chicken breasts
½ cup Chinese sweet chili sauce
2 cups of jasmine rice cooked according to
    directions
1 jar of artichoke hearts, rinsed and drained
Juice of 1 lemon
1 can of coconut milk

Marinate chicken in Chinese sweet chili sauce overnight. Cook chicken until done. Cool and cut into bite size pieces.

Rinse artichoke hearts and toss with the lemon juice.

Heat coconut milk over very low heat.

Rinse rice before cooking. When rice is cooked, pour coconut milk over rice and stir in completely, then cover and let stand 5 minutes.

Combine all the ingredients together in a large bowl and chill thoroughly.

Serves 8 as a side dish, 4 as a main course

Watermelon and Feta Salad

This may look like an unlikely combination, but trust me, it's a winner. This a great summer salad with a creative twist or two. The mint flowers add a special zip…and then there's the feta cheese. Some people are put off when they hear that there's feta in the salad, but once they taste it, they love it. Feta comes in many varieties, the mildest being Croation feta, so you can adjust the recipe according to your taste.

1 medium red onion, minced
2 – 4 limes, depending on juiciness
3½ pounds ripe watermelon, cut from rind, seeds removed
10 ounces feta cheese
3 – 4 tablespoons extra virgin olive oil
1 bunch flat leaf parsley
1 bunch fresh spearmint (leaves and/or flowers), chopped
   coarsely*

Peel and halve the onion, cut into very fine slices and place in a bowl. Squeeze limes over the onion and set aside until ready to use.

Cut watermelon into bite-size pieces and place in a large bowl. Gently crumble the feta cheese all over the watermelon.

Tear sprigs of parsley so that you have the entire leaf and add to the watermelon. Add the chopped mint at this time. Pour the minced onions and lime juice all over the salad, add the oil and very gently toss the salad with your hands, taking care not to break up the watermelon or feta. Add fresh black pepper (and if desired, some black olives) and serve.

Serves 6 – 8

*It is easier to use a pair of scissors and cut the flowers and spearmint leaves.

Marigold Tofu "Eggless" Egg Salad

My friend and professional chef Alyson Crispin developed this recipe for the book. I have to say that even I, the carnivore, will be making this. Signet marigolds used in the recipe have a lemony scent that adds another layer of flavor to the "eggless" salad.

1 package firm tofu
2 tablespoons olive oil
1 tablespoon vinegar
1 tablespoon mustard
2 tablespoons chopped pickle, sweet or dill
1 tablespoon diced sweet onion
½ teaspoon salt
½ teaspoon pepper
½ teaspoon cumin
3 tablespoons diced or snipped marigold petals

In a large bowl, combine all ingredients except the tofu. Crumble the tofu and add into the bowl. Using a fork, mix around until blended. You can add a bit of your favorite mayonnaise if you like.

Chill for at least one hour for the flavors to bloom.

Makes about 3 – 4 servings.

Oriental Broccoli Salad

This wonderful, colorful salad is ideal for a summer picnic. Make it simply veggie, or toss in some shredded or diced chicken before you serve. The sesame vinaigrette dressing will make it a standout.

½ cup slivered or sliced almonds
2 tablespoon sesame seeds
1 head of broccoli, florets only, broken apart
¾ pound bean sprouts
2 cups sliced fresh mushrooms
2 green onions, chopped thinly, including green stems
½ small cucumber, peeled, seeded and diced
1½ cups shredded red cabbage
¼ cup sunflower seeds
1 package ramen noodles, broken up

Dressing
½ cup vegetable oil
3 tablespoon rice vinegar
2 tablespoon light or low sodium soy sauce
1 tablespoon granulated sugar
1½ teaspoon sesame oil
1 clove garlic, minced
Salt and pepper to taste

Toast almonds and sesame seeds in a pan over medium heat, stirring occasionally until fragrant. Let cool. Toss rest of ingredients together except for ramen noodles and add almonds and sesame seeds. Refrigerate up to 4 hours before serving.

Whisk together all ingredients for dressing and refrigerate up to 4 hours before serving. Add dressing before serving. Sprinkle with broken ramen noodles.

Serves 4 as a side salad or 2 as an entrée.

ENTREES

Lemon Verbena Salmon

Lemon verbena is so versatile that I can't resist adding it so many dishes. Here it takes the place of the usual citrus addition after the fact, permeating the fish while it's cooking.

1 cup canola oil
10 lemon verbena leaves or a handful of the flowers (or a combination), freshly torn
4 salmon fillets
1 tablespoon fresh dill, snipped fine

The night before, combine the oil and verbena and refrigerate. Brush the salmon on both sides with the lemon verbena oil and place on a broiler pan. Place under broiler for approximately 6 minutes on each side. Remove from pan and sprinkle with fresh dill weed.

Serves 4

Salmon Pizza with Nasturtiums

This recipe was inspired by the traditional lox and bagels. You can use it as an appetizer or eat it as cool summer dinner.

1 14-inch prepared pizza crust
6 ounces thinly sliced smoked salmon
   or 1 cooked salmon filet (I like to grill it
   with a little butter & brown sugar)
4 ounces cream cheese, softened
4 ounces sour cream
¼ cup finely chopped red onion
¼ cup nasturtiums, flowers and leaves
1 tablespoon or more of chopped
   nasturtiums for garnish

Combine cream cheese and sour cream until smooth. Finely chop nasturtiums and add to cheese mixture. Let it sit for one hour in the refrigerator. Spread the cheese mixture over the pizza crust. Flake cooked salmon or slices of smoked salmon uniformly over the crust then sprinkle with the red onion and the rest of nasturtiums. Cut in wedges or squares and serve cold.

Serves 10–12 as an appetizer or for 4 persons, 2 slices each.

Chicken with Herbes de Provence

The herbal and floral flavors of herbes de Provence were destined to be used with poultry. This seasoning is the standard in many dishes in southern France. The herbs themselves have an affinity for poultry, pork and lamb. It should always be added to the dish while cooking, so the oils are released into the recipe. Combine this entrée with roasted potatoes or other vegetables and a nice white wine, and you can transport yourself to a French bistro for dinner.

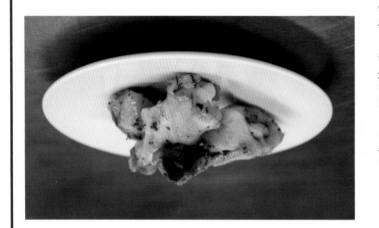

4 chicken breasts or thighs, with skin
1 tablespoon herbes de Provence
½ cup extra virgin olive oil

Clean and dry chicken and place in a bowl. Leave skin on. Skin helps prevent loss of moisture and improves flavor. You can always take it off after cooking.

Mix herbes de Provence into olive oil and allow it to sit for 4 hours or longer. You can make this up to a week ahead of time. Pour oil over chicken and marinate for a couple of hours in the refrigerator.

Place chicken on baking rack and cook at 350° F for 25 – 30 minutes or until juices run clear.

Serves 4.

Asian Noodles Vinaigrette with Nasturtiums

This recipe came to me after I had sampled a cold noodle dish at a friend's house. The simplicity of the dish requires cooking only the noodles and dressing it with an Asian style vinaigrette that is slightly sweet with a little heat. The natural peppery flavor of nasturtiums makes in an ideal flower to add to the noodles.

⅓ cup rice vinegar
1 teaspoon sugar
2 tablespoons fresh ginger, peeled and grated
1 tablespoon honey
2 teaspoons sesame oil
2 teaspoons Chinese sweet chili pepper sauce
¼ cup canola oil

1 pound cooked linguini
1 carrot, peeled and grated
1 red bell pepper, seeded and julienned
½ small cucumber
3 green onions, sliced on the diagonal
1 cup nasturtium flowers and leaves, chopped
¼ cup chopped fresh parsley or cilantro leaves

Whisk together vinegar, sugar, ginger, honey, sesame oil and sweet chili pepper sauce. Slowly whisk in canola oil until combined.

Add cooked noodles, carrot, pepper, cucumber, green onions, nasturtiums and parsley/cilantro. Gently toss and serve.

Serves 6

ENTREES

Sunny Shrimp

This quick and easy dish invites the oohs and ahhs with its wonderful tropical flavor of pineapple sage. It really doesn't get any easier than this.

1 pound raw shrimp, cleaned and deveined
5 leaves of pineapple sage or a handful of sage flowers (or a combination), chopped or torn fine
1 small can crushed pineapple in its own juice, drained, reserving juice.
1 tablespoon canola oil

In a bowl combine shrimp, pineapple juice and pineapple sage and let marinate for 2 – 3 hours.

Heat oil in large frying pan and add shrimp combination. Stir in crushed pineapple. Cook until shrimp become pink. Remove from heat and serve.

Serves 4

Chocolate Pavlova with Strawberries and Rosewater

There is nothing quite like a filled chocolate Pavlova to give you the ultimate satisfaction on your tongue – a perfect combination of flavors for a sinfully rich, exquisite dessert that will delight everyone and make you look like the queen of desserts! This is really easy and so to die for!

Meringue
6 large egg whites at room temperature
1 cup sugar
1 teaspoon white or balsamic vinegar
3 tablespoons Dutch processed cocoa powder
2 ounce ssemi-sweet or bittersweet chocolate, chopped

Topping
1 cup heavy whipping cream (at least 36% heavy cream)
1 tablespoon granulated white sugar
Coarsely grated chocolate or candied rose petals, for
   sprinkling

Fruit
Fresh strawberries
½ teaspoon rosewater

Hull and cut fresh strawberries and place in a bowl. Stir in the rosewater. Let strawberries marinate for an hour or so before using.

DESSERTS

Preheat oven to 350° F and place rack in center of oven. Line a cookie sheet with parchment paper and draw an 8-inch circle (using a cake pan or a dish) onto the parchment paper.

In a small bowl sift together cocoa and cornstarch and set aside.

With an electric mixer, whisk egg whites. Beat on medium high until egg whites hold soft peaks. Start adding the sugar, a tablespoon at a time, and continue to beat until the meringue holds stiff peaks. Fold in vinegar. Sprinkle cocoa mixture over egg whites and gently fold into the mixture.

Gently fold in chopped chocolate. Spread the meringue inside the circle drawn on the parchment paper, smoothing around the edges. Place in oven and immediately turn down heat to 300° F. Bake for about 1¼ – 1½ hours or until the outside is dry. Leave the door slightly open and let the meringue cool completely in the oven.

Prepare topping

In a cold bowl, beat whipping cream with sugar until stiff peaks form.

To assemble

Place meringue on serving dish. Top with whipped cream and spoon marinated strawberries over top of whipped cream and serve. Sprinkle with grated chocolate or candied rose petals.

Serves 8

75

Strawberry Lavender Delight

Strawberries and lavender are great companions in this light dessert. The lavender counters the sweetness of the strawberry flavor while adding its own scent. Easy to make, it's ideal for a summer picnic.

1 large box strawberry gelatin
2 cups boiling hot water
5 washed and dried lavender stems, no flowers
1 cup lavender syrup*

1 ½ cups cold water
1 8-ounce container of Cool Whip
1 pint strawberries, washed and sliced

Place lavender stems in bowl. Dissolve gelatin in hot water with lavender stems. Remove lavender stems. Add cold water. Thicken in refrigerator until the consistency of egg whites. Whip for 2 minutes, then add Cool Whip and beat 2-3 minutes more. Pour into an 8 x 8 pan.

Wash and slice strawberries. Pour syrup over strawberries and let it sit for half an hour. Drain. Spoon strawberry/lavender mixture carefully over gelatin. Chill until firm.

*See recipe for Lavender Syrup on p. 84

DESSERTS

Rose Petal Ice Cream

Nothing can compare to the ice cream in Europe with its extremely rich butterfat content and creamy texture. This is my humble attempt to recreate the ice cream that first introduced me to the wonderful world of edible flowers.

1 gallon French vanilla ice cream (softened slightly)
2 – 3 tablespoons rose syrup
1 teaspoon rose water
1 cup fresh fragrant rose petals, chopped fine
or
1 cup dried fragrant rose petals, crushed
1 cup chopped pistachios, if desired

Add rose syrup and rose water to softened ice cream and blend thoroughly. Add rose petals and pistachios. Refreeze until hard.

You may serve the ice cream with a few fresh rose petals on top.

Floral Liqueurs
Basic Recipe

Making your own floral liqueurs requires patience. The results will be well worth the wait. Some flowers you could use would be elderberry, orange or lemon blossoms, hibiscus blossoms, dandelions, mint flowers, lavender, blueberry, and roses. Or, in lieu of flowers, you can make this recipe with fruits and berries. The end result will be a lovely after-dinner drink, especially on a hot summer's day.

1 cup tightly packed flowers, freshly picked
(or, instead of flowers, you can use 16 ounces berries or fruit)
3 cups 80-proof good quality vodka
1¼ cups granulated sugar

Wash and dry the flowers (or berries/fruit – slightly crush fruit if small). Place them in a container and add vodka. Place in a covered container in a cool, dark place, stirring once a week for 2 – 4 weeks. Strain through a metal sieve lined with a coffee filter or a jelly bag. Transfer the unsweetened liqueur to a glass bottle or jar with tight cap. To every 3 cups of unsweetened liqueur add 1¼ cup granulated sugar and stir. Let it rest for at least 3

Dandelion Liqueur

months in a cool dark place again. Through a lined sieve, carefully strain the clear liqueur to a new bottle or jar. Add more sugar if necessary. If the liqueur is too strong you may dilute it with a little fruit juice or water.

Note: If you use lavender, be aware that its flavor is potent, so you may want to reduce the amount in the recipe.

DRINKS

Malibu Margarita

This is just a new twist on an old drink. Strawberries and lavender go hand in hand, and as a drink it becomes a refreshing beverage on a hot summer's day. A little liquor added only makes it more relaxing.

1 cup pureed strawberries
4 cups cold water
¼ cup rum (optional)
Sugar (for dipping the glass in)

The Syrup

1½ cups sugar
1½ cups water
2 tablespoons dried or fresh lavender blossoms and/or leaves

Place syrup ingredients in a saucepan and boil until thick and syrupy. Pour through a strainer and let cool. In a shallow bowl, reserve 1 cup and set aside.

Take a margarita glass or any other glass you may choose, and dip the rim into the reserved bowl of the syrup. Then dip the glass into sugar, rimming the glass with sugar. Let the glass dry upright for a few minutes. Mix the rest of the syrup, strawberry puree, water and rum in a pitcher and pour over ice.

Serves 4 – 6

Pineapple Guava Frozen Smoothie

Pineapple guava flowers have a taste that has been described as a cross between the guava fruit and cotton candy so there is no need to add sugar to the recipe. Kids will get a serving of dairy and fruit with no sugar or fat added.

1½ cups pineapple guava flowers, lightly packed
1½ cups frozen strawberries
1½ cups chilled plain yogurt

Place frozen strawberries in a blender or smoothie maker and pulse until almost smooth. Add pineapple guava flowers and pulse until smooth. Add yogurt and blend until combined. Pour into parfait glasses and freeze until solid. You can also make smoothie popsicles for the kids in popsicle holders. Just fill the holders ¾ full, place cover over holders and add sticks. Freeze until firm.

Makes about 4 8-ounce smoothies or 8 4-ounce smoothies. The number of popsicles depends on the size of the popsicle holders.

BUTTERS

FLORAL BUTTERS
Basic Recipe

Butters are an easy way to add floral accents to your food without a lot of fuss. The flower should match the food you are serving. Feel free to experiment. Butters can be made sweet or savory. Always start off with the lower amount of flower since some can be quite strong (especially lavender, monarda and lemon verbena). Use them on toast, on meat and fish or incorporate it into your baking if the recipe calls for butter and the flavor would match. Lavender butter and a sugar cookie recipe would be a lovely match. Melted lavender butter could be drizzled over a smoked pork chop. Chive flower butter on toast topped with a poached egg is a great twist on an old and sometimes bland dish.

Simply combine a stick of real butter, softened, with one of the following:

Calendula petals: ½ cup, minced

Chive Flower: 1 floret fresh, minced

Edible flower mix (dried): 2 teaspoons, finely crumbled

Lavender: 1 tablespoon fresh flowers and/or finely minced leaves — or ¼ tablespoon dried lavender

Lemon verbena: 1 teaspoon finely minced flowers and/or leaves

Monarda (bee balm): 1 tablespoon fresh, minced — or 1 teaspoon crumbled dried monarda

Nasturtiums: 1 ½ tablespoons fresh, minced, flowers and/or leaves.

Pineapple sage: 1 teaspoon leaves or flowers, finely minced
Rose petals: 2 tablespoons fresh, minced, with white heels removed –
  or 1 tablespoon dried, finely crumbled
Thyme, basil or oregano flowers: 1 teaspoon, minced

Mix with a spoon or hand mixer. If you like, you can use butter molds and keep in the freezer until ready to serve. Or refrigerate and use within a week.

Be aware that...

Lilacs do not make a good butter. Their fleshy flowers can become quite nasty looking and discolored. Lilacs are best used in a syrup.

SYRUPS

Basic Recipe

Syrups are easy to make and versatile in their use. As with all fresh flowers, harvest them early in the day and carefully dry off the morning dew. Favorite flowers for syrups are lavender, rose petals, lilacs, anise hyssop, pansy, dandelion, borage, any of the mints, monarda, lemon verbena and lemon balm.

1 cup water

1 cup granulated sugar

Flowers and/or stems (from ½ cup to just a few leaves or stems, depending on the flower or stem)

Add your flowers/stems, stir and boil down until thick. Strain out flowers and let cool.

Serve over your wildest imagination……pancakes, crepes, fruit, ice cream, teas, lemonades, champagne and more.

One note about making syrups: Many flowers turn an odd color while cooking and have a gray-green look to them, which isn't very appetizing. Lilacs and lavender benefit from a few blueberries being added to the syrup; this adds color without flavor. If you're using a fragrant rose that is white, pink or yellow, a couple of raspberries or strawberries will improve the color. Why use food dye when there are better options?

Lavender syrup

(for Strawberry Lavender Delight Dessert)

1 cup sugar
1 cup water
5 stems lavender – or 2 tablespoons
   dried lavender buds

Combine in small saucepan until boiling and reduced by half. Let cool. Strain out lavender buds if necessary.

Wash and slice strawberries. Pour syrup over strawberries and let it sit for half an hour. Then drain and add strawberries to gelatin mixture in pan.

SYRUPS

Pansy syrup

2 cups granulated sugar
1 cup water
1 cup dark pansy petals, loosely packed

Put pansy petals into a food processor with a steel blade. Add ⅓ cup sugar and grind pansies into the sugar by pulsing 4 or 5 times, then process for about 30 seconds.

In a small non-aluminum saucepan combine rest of sugar, pansy/sugar mixture and water. Over medium heat bring the mixture to a boil. Stir once and reduce the heat to low. Allow to simmer and cook to syrup stage (or not go over 220° F on a candy thermometer). Remove from heat and pour into a heatproof container. Allow to cool, then store in the refrigerator for a week.

SUGARS
Basic Recipe

Sugars can be used to mix in drinks, cooking or baking. They are one of the easiest things to do with edible flowers and will add a delicate flavor. Of course you don't want to use something like a peppery-flavored nasturtium in sugar. I don't think your tea or cookies would taste quite right! Use the same flowers as for a flower syrup, including lavender, rose petals, lilacs, anise hyssop, pansy, borage, any of the mints, monarda, lemon verbena and lemon balm.

1 cup granulated sugar
Flowers and/or stems, whole or slightly torn (see quantities below)

You may want to experiment with the amounts of flowers, from using ½ cup of flowers for lilacs and roses, to a few stems of lavender or hyssop…to just a few leaves from the mints and other herbs.

Mix your flowers/stems into a cup of granulated sugr and allow to sit for a couple of weeks in a closed container. Stir it every couple of days since the sugar will naturally draw moisture out of the flowers and clump a bit. After a couple of weeks, remove the flowers by simply sifting them out of the sugar. You can add the sugar to drinks such as lemonade or tea or you can use it in your cooking and baking.

RESOURCES

I find many edible flowers in local specialty stores such as Asian markets, Middle Eastern stores and others. These markets usually have rose syrups, dried roses, rose paste and much, much more. Also, specialty food markets and farmers markets are able to supply edible flowers, either fresh or dried.

Some of my favorites (they all ship):

The Village Herb Shop
Edible flower mixture and other dried flowers and herbs
17 East Orange St.
Chagrin Falls, Ohio 44022
440-247-5029
www.villageherbshop.com

Crystallized Flower Company
Crystallized organic flowers
Karen Toocheck
Willoughby, Ohio 44094
440-478-5302
karen@crystallizedflowerco.com

Penzeys Spices
Lavender, juniper berries, Herbes de Provence and other dried herbs and mixtures
800-741-7787
www.Penzeys.com

Monin syrup
Rose syrup, violet syrup
800-966-5225
www.monin.com

Grocery Chains

Whole Foods Market
Various organic flowers and dried spices and flowers; varies by store.
www.wholefoodsmarket.com

Trader Joe's
Various organic flowers; varies by store
www.traderjoes.com

Note: None of these companies has paid to be on this list.

Edible Flower Information Online

www.extension.iastate.edu/Publications/RG302.pdf
www.ces.ncsu.edu/depts/hort/hil/hil-8513.html
www.ext.colostate.edu/PUBS/GARDEN/07237.html

Poison Control Centers

Call 800-222-1222 if you think you or someone else has been poisoned. This is the American Association of Poison Control Centers national number for reaching all 62 poison control centers in the United States, Virgin Islands, and Puerto Rico.

87

INDEX

(Note: flowers shown in bold are **not** edible)

Anise hyssop 2, 83
Apple blossom 3
Artichoke 4, 54, 65
Azalea iv
Bachelor button 5
Basil 6, 20, 22, 62, 63, 82
Bee balm v, 31, 56, 81
Borage 7, 83, 86
Boxwood iv
Broccoli ii, 8, 10, 50, 68
Burning bush iv
Butters 9, 45, 51, 53, 81, 82
Caladium iv
Calendula 9, 56, 60, 81, 89
Cauliflower 8, 10
Chamomile 11
Chicken 4, 22, 52, 57, 59, 64, 65, 68, 71, 89
Chive 12, 63, 81
Clematis iv
Cornflower 5
Cosmos iv
Daffodil iv
Dandelion ii, 13, 78, 83
Daylily 14
Delphinium iv

Dianthus 15, 56
Eastern Redbud 16
Elephant ears iv
Elderberry 17, 78
False Red Yucca 18
Fennel 19, 22
Four o'clocks iv
Foxglove iv
Garlic 20, 57, 61, 68
Geraniums 21
Herbes de Provence 22, 71, 87
Hibiscus 23, 78
Hyacinth iv
Hydrangea iv
Iris iv
Ivy iv
Jack in the pulpit iv
Lantana iv
Lavender v, 5, 22, 24, 56, 59, 76, 78, 79, 81, 83, 84, 91
Lemon balm 25, 83, 86
Lemon verbena 26, 81, 83, 86, 69
Lilac 27, 82, 83, 86
Lily of the valley iv
Lobelia iv
Marjoram 22, 29, 30

Mint 30, 35, 40, 51, 56, 62, 66, 78, 83, 86
Monarda 31, 56, 81, 83, 86
Morning glory iv
Mountain laurel iv
Mrs. Know-It-All 91
Nasturtium 32, 56, 57, 63, 64, 70, 72, 81, 86
Oleander iv
Onion flower 33, 61
Orange blossom 34, 78
Oregano 22, 29, 30 35, 82
Organic iii, 44, 87, 91
Pansy 36, 83, 85, 86
Passionflower 37
Pea, Garden pea 38
Periwinkle iv
pesticides iii, 13
Pineapple guava 39, 80
Pineapple sage 40, 73, 82
Pistil iii, v
Prickly pear 41
Privet iv
Radish 42
Rhododendron iv
Rose i, ii, v, 21, 23, 43, 44, 56, 58, 74, 75, 77, 78, 82, 83, 86, 87
Rose hips 43, 44

Rosemary ii, 22, 30, 45, 62
Sage, Garden sage ii, 46
Scape 20
Scarlet runner bean 47
Signet marigold 28, 67
Squash, squash flower 48
Stamen iii, v
Strawberry 24, 49, 76, 79, 84
Sugar, Sugars 18, 23, 39, 45, 58, 59, 60, 72, 74, 75, 79, 80, 81, 83, 84, 85, 86
Sunflower ii, 50, 68
Sweet pea iv
Syrup, Syrups 2, 7, 13, 24, 25, 26, 27, 31, 36, 49, 76, 77, 79, 82, 85, 87
Thyme ii, 22, 51, 62, 64, 82
Tulip v, 52
Vinaigrette 18, 32, 68, 72
Viola 36, 53
Wisteria iv
Yucca 18, 54

RECIPES

ACCENTS
Edible Flower Cream
  Cheese Spread 56
Fresh Salsa with Pineapple
  and Nasturtiums 32, 57
Rose Petal Jam ii, 44, 58
Caramelized Onions with
  Lavender 24, 59

APPETIZERS & SIDE DISHES
Calendula Corn Muffins
  9, 60
Oven Roasted Italian
  Green Beans with Onion
  Flowers 33, 61
Mushrooms Stuffed with
  Fresh Mozzarella and
  Thyme 51, 62
Nasturtium Bundles 32, 63
Roasted Red Pepper Soup
  with Nasturtium and
  Thyme 64

SALADS
Artichoke Chicken Salad with
  Jasmine Rice 4, 65
Watermelon and Feta Salad
  30, 66
Marigold Tofu "Eggless" Egg
  Salad 28, 67
Oriental Broccoli Salad 8,
  50, 68

ENTREES
Lemon Verbena Salmon 26,
  69
Asian Noodles Vinaigrette with
  Nasturtiums 32, 72
Chicken Herbes de Provence
  71
Salmon Pizza with Nasturtiums
  70, 22
Sunny Shrimp 40, 73

DESSERTS
Chocolate Pavlova with
  Strawberries and Rosewater
  74, 75
Strawberry Lavender Delight
  24, 76, 84
Rose Petal Ice Cream i, 44, 77

DRINKS
Floral Liqueurs 78
Malibu Margarita 24, 79
Pineapple Guava Frozen
  Smoothie 80

BUTTERS 9, 44, 51, 53, 81

SYRUPS 26, 49, 83, 87,
Lavender Syrup 24, 76, 84
Pansy Syrup 36, 85

SUGARS 86

ACKNOWLEDGMENTS

None of this is ever possible without the help of family, friends, acquaintances and sometimes strangers. So thank you to my family, including my husband Don and my daughter Regan, who have helped me keep my sanity not only while writing this book but for the years of help at my edible flowers food fests.

Thank you to Paul Kelly and Cathy Dees from St. Lynn's Press, who helped me conceive and deliver this book.

Special thanks to my contributors and brainstormers, who have made these recipes successes: Suzanne Carney, Alyson Crispin, Mary Elabarger, Lyn Lang, Susan Marquesen, and Martha Swiss

To Patti McCormick, my main photographer: Your creative eye made the photos works of art.

Thanks and appreciation to Allegheny County Parks, Sandy Feather, Penn State Master Gardeners, Allegheny County, Doug Oster, Chef Jeffrey Ward, Jimmie Turner, Stephanie Cohen, Delena Tull, Cathy Wilkinson Barash, Bill Yates, Barbara Bane, Arlene Burnett, Judith McLaughlin McGinnis, Kathleen Gips, Cyndi Lauderdale, Lisa Marini Finerty, Raymond Schreiber, Kenny Point, Nick Federoff.

ABOUT THE AUTHOR

Denise Schreiber lives and gardens in a Pittsburgh suburb with her husband, daughter and four cats. The granddaughter of Italian farmer immigrants whose last name actually means "To work with tools of the earth," her earliest memories are of being in the family garden, pulling carrots out of the ground and washing them off with a hose, the foliage still attached.

A lifelong gardener with a degree in floriculture and liberal studies, Denise is the Greenhouse Manager for Allegheny County Parks. She is also a prize-winning baker and preserver. She began experimenting with edible flowers after a trip to the gardens of Great Britain. In 2000 she started the popular Edible Flowers Food Fest, held in Pittsburgh every July, featuring tastings of a wide array of flower recipes.

Many people in the Pittsburgh area are familiar with Denise as the expert gardener "Mrs. Know-It-All," a fixture on the widely-heard KDKA Sunday morning radio show The Organic Gardeners.

More of Denise's edible flowers recipes and tips can be found online at www.edibleflowers1.com.

ABOUT THE PRINCIPAL PHOTOGRAPHER

The good-enough-to-eat food photos and many of the flower photos are by Patricia Toth McCormick, a Pittsburgh-area photographer who specializes in images from nature, garden portraits and expressive lifestyle portraiture. Patricia holds a Fine Arts degree from Carnegie Mellon University. More information about her work can be found online at www.patriciatothmccormick.com.